potatoes

simple and delicious easy–to–make recipes

Susanna Tee

p

This is a Parragon Publishing Book
This edition published in 2002

Parragon Publishing
Queen Street House
4 Queen Street
Bath BA1 1HE
United Kingdom

ISBN: 0-75258-719-6

Printed in China

Produced by The Bridgewater Book Company Ltd

Creative Director Terry Jeavons
Art Director Sarah Howerd
Editorial Director Fiona Biggs
Senior Editor Mark Truman
Assistant Editor Tom Kitch
Photographer Ian Parsons
Home Economist Annabel Hartog
Page Make-up Chris and Jane Lanaway

COVER
Photographer Ian Parsons
Home Economist Sara Hesketh

NOTES FOR THE READER

- This book uses both imperial and metric measurements. Follow the same units of measurement
  throughout; do not mix imperial and metric.
- All spoon measurements are level: teaspoons are assumed to be 5 ml, and tablespoons are
  assumed to be 15 ml.
- Unless otherwise stated, milk is assumed to be full fat, eggs are large, individual vegetables, such as
  potatoes, are medium, and pepper is freshly ground black pepper.
- Recipes using raw or very lightly cooked eggs should be avoided by infants, the elderly, pregnant
  women, convalescents, and anyone suffering from an illness.
- Optional ingredients, variations, or serving suggestions have not been included in the calculations.
  The times given are an approximate guide only. Preparation times differ according to the techniques
  used by different people and the cooking times vary as a result of the type of oven used.

contents

introduction

Potatoes originated from Peru, where the small brown tubers, barely resembling the vegetable that we know today, were eaten raw. Now they are found all over the world and are a staple part of our diet, used many different ways—baked, fried, boiled, roasted, mashed, or as an ingredient in pies, stews, and casseroles.

Potatoes come in different varieties, colors, and shapes. Once they are cooked, their texture varies from waxy to mealy. Waxy potatoes (often sold under the name of salad potatoes) and new potatoes are firmer and hold their shape when cooked. Mealy potatoes, on the other hand, are softer and break up more easily when cooked, so they are better for fluffy roast potatoes and for mashing. Reliable mealy potatoes include the King Edward, Maris Piper, and the red-skinned Desirée and Romano.

Nevertheless, all potatoes do have one thing in common: they are so versatile that they can be made into hundreds of exciting dishes. This book is filled with imaginative recipes, but without complicated cooking methods, for soups, salads, accompaniments, lunch, and more substantial supper dishes. There is no longer any excuse for reaching for a bag of frozen fries—incidentally, the French fry is the largest selling frozen vegetable in the world! There is something here for everyone.

guide to recipe key		
	easy	Recipes are graded as follows: 1 pea = easy; 2 peas = very easy; 3 peas = extremely easy.
	serves 4	Recipes generally serve four people. Simply halve the ingredients to serve two, taking care not to mix imperial and metric measurements.
	15 minutes	Preparation time. Where chilling is involved, this time has been added on separately: eg, 15 minutes + 30 minutes to chill.
	15 minutes	Cooking time.

vichyssoise
page 16

potato wedges with apricots & walnuts
page 32

homemade oven french fries
page 52

spanish omelet
page 68

homemade soups

Perhaps the simplest use of the potato is in soups—these can range from the most frugal, such as Fresh Broccoli Soup, to the more sophisticated, such as the classic Vichyssoise. Potato soups are also versatile: they may be hot, thick chowders for a cold winter's day, or chilled and light for a summer's evening. Additionally, they can be served as a simple appetizer or as a more substantial main course. All, however, are easy to prepare, as you will find in the small selection in this chapter.

smoked cod chowder

		ingredients	
extremely easy		2 tbsp butter	1¼ cups boiling water
		1 onion, finely chopped	salt and pepper
serves 4		1 small celery stalk, finely diced	12 oz/350 g smoked cod fillets,
		1 cup diced potatoes	cut into bite-size pieces
		⅓ cup diced carrots	1¼ cups milk
10 minutes			
30 minutes			

Melt the butter in a large pan over low heat. Add the onion and celery and cook for 5 minutes, until softened but not brown.

Add the potatoes, carrots, water, salt, and pepper. Bring to a boil, then reduce the heat, and simmer for about 10 minutes, or until the vegetables are tender. Add the fish to the chowder and cook for a further 10 minutes.

Pour in the milk and heat gently. Season to taste and serve hot.

fresh broccoli soup

very easy	
serves 4	
10 minutes	
35–40 minutes	

ingredients

2 tbsp butter
1 large onion, chopped
9 oz/250 g potatoes, peeled and diced
2½ cups chicken bouillon

1 medium head broccoli,
    cut into florets
salt and pepper

chopped fresh parsley, to garnish

Melt the butter in a large pan over low heat, then add the onion, and cook for about 10 minutes, or until softened.

Add the potatoes and chicken bouillon, bring to a boil, then reduce the heat, and simmer for 15 minutes.

Remove from the heat, let cool slightly, then pour one-third into a food processor. Blend the soup in the food processor until smooth, then return to the pan with the reserved soup.

Add the broccoli, salt, and pepper. Bring back to a boil, then reduce the heat, and simmer for 10–15 minutes.

Serve garnished with parsley.

thai-style pork
& cabbage soup

		ingredients	
extremely easy		1 lb/450 g pork tenderloin	1²⁄₃ cups diced potatoes
		2 tbsp butter	salt and pepper
serves 4		1 onion, chopped finely	1 tsp lemon juice
		1 tbsp finely chopped ginger root	3 tbsp chopped fresh parsley
		3³⁄₄ cups shredded green cabbage	
15 minutes		5 cups chicken or	
		vegetable bouillon	
30 minutes			

Cut the pork into small strips.

Melt the butter in a large pan over low heat. Add the onion and cook for about 3 minutes, stirring, until beginning to soften. Stir in the ginger and cabbage and cook for a further minute.

Add the bouillon, potatoes, salt, and pepper. Bring to a boil, then simmer for about 10 minutes, or until the potatoes are tender.

Stir in the pork and cook for about 5 minutes, or until the pork is tender. Stir in the lemon juice and parsley and serve hot.

cullen skink

		ingredients
easy		1 lb/450 g potatoes, peeled and cut into chunks 1¼ cups boiling water
serves 4		2 tbsp butter 2 cups milk 1 onion, finely chopped salt and pepper 12 oz/350 g smoked haddock, skinned chopped fresh chives, to garnish
15 minutes		
25 minutes		

Cook the potatoes in a pan of salted boiling water for about 20 minutes, or until tender.

Meanwhile, melt the butter in a large pan. Add the onion and cook for about 5 minutes, or until soft. Add the haddock and boiling water and simmer for about 10 minutes, or until it is just tender.

Using a slotted spoon, remove the fish from the pan and then break into bite-size pieces, discarding any bones.

Drain the cooked potatoes and mash them. Gradually stir the potatoes into the cooking liquid, then slowly add the milk. Bring to a boil and then simmer for 2–3 minutes to heat through. Stir in the fish and season with salt and pepper.

Serve hot, garnished with chives.

vichyssoise

		ingredients	
easy		2 tbsp butter	chopped fresh chives, to garnish
		1 onion, chopped	
serves 4		1 lb/450 g leeks, thinly sliced	$^2/_3$ cup light cream, to serve
		1 lb/450 g potatoes, peeled and cubed	
		4 cups chicken bouillon	
10 minutes + 4 hours to chill		salt and pepper	
40 minutes			

Melt the butter in a large pan. Add the onion and leeks and cook for about 10 minutes, or until soft but not colored.

Add the potatoes, bouillon, salt, and pepper. Bring to a boil, then cover the pan, and simmer for about 30 minutes, or until the vegetables are very tender.

Let cool slightly, then pour the soup into a food processor, and blend until smooth.

Chill the soup in the refrigerator for at least 4 hours. To serve, stir in the cream, adjust the seasoning, and garnish with chives.

fresh potato salads

Salads are where new potatoes come into their own. Their firm texture makes them ideal for boiling because they keep their shape so well. If new potatoes are not in season, you can always use waxy potatoes or specialty salad potatoes in these recipes. Potato salads don't consist merely of chopped potatoes tossed in mayonnaise. These recipes are far from boring—some are chilled, some are warm, but all are bursting with flavor and freshness.

roast potato salad

	ingredients	
extremely easy	1 lb/450 g new potatoes	3 tbsp chopped fresh parsley leaves
	6 tbsp olive oil	12 cherry tomatoes, halved
serves 4	1 garlic clove, crushed	½ cucumber, diced and unpeeled
	salt and pepper	1 orange bell pepper, cored, seeded,
	1 tbsp red wine vinegar	and diced
15 minutes + 1 hour to chill	1 tsp white sugar	4 scallions, sliced thinly
45 minutes		

Preheat the oven to 400°F/200°C. Spread out the potatoes in a large roasting pan. Combine 4 tablespoons of the olive oil with the garlic, salt, and pepper, and drizzle it over the potatoes. Transfer to the preheated oven and roast for about 45 minutes, turning once or twice during cooking, until they are tender and golden brown.

Meanwhile, make a dressing by combining the remaining oil with the vinegar, sugar, and parsley. Season to taste.

When the potatoes are cooked, remove them from the oven, let cool completely, and put into a salad bowl. Add the tomatoes, cucumber, orange bell pepper, and scallions and toss together.

Drizzle the dressing over the salad and toss again. Cover with plastic wrap and chill in the refrigerator before serving.

blackened potato
& fennel salad

very easy	
serves 4	
10 minutes	
20–25 minutes	

ingredients

1 lb/450 g small new potatoes
1 fennel bulb, quartered lengthwise
6 tbsp olive oil
1 red bell pepper, cored, seeded,
   and diced
4 tbsp white wine vinegar
salt and pepper

½ cup pitted black olives
2 shallots, chopped finely

3 tbsp chopped fresh cilantro leaves,
   to garnish

Preheat the broiler. Preheat the oven to 400°F/200°C. Toss the potatoes and fennel quarters in half of the oil, then put in the broiler pan in a single layer. Add the red bell pepper and broil for about 5 minutes, turning once, until slightly charred and the bell pepper skins have blistered. Transfer to the oven and cook for 15–20 minutes, or until tender.

Meanwhile, combine the remaining oil, vinegar, salt, and pepper.

When cool enough to handle, cut the potatoes and fennel into ½ inch/1 cm dice and put in a salad bowl. Add the olives, shallots, and red bell pepper, then toss together.

Drizzle the dressing over the salad and toss again. Sprinkle with the cilantro. Serve warm.

baby potato
& sun-dried tomato salad

easy	
serves 4	
10 minutes + 1 hour to chill	
15 minutes	

ingredients

1 lb/450 g small new potatoes
¼ cup sun-dried tomatoes
scant ½ cup plain yogurt
salt and pepper

1 tbsp olive oil
⅔ cup celery, sliced
2 scallions, sliced
1 medium carrot, grated

Cook the potatoes in salted boiling water for about 15 minutes, or until they are tender.

Meanwhile, put the tomatoes in a bowl, cover with boiling water, and let stand for 10 minutes. Mix the yogurt, salt, and pepper.

Drain the cooked potatoes and put in a salad bowl. Add the olive oil and toss together. Drain the tomatoes and slice thinly. Add to the potatoes with the celery, scallions, and carrot.

Drizzle the dressing over the salad and toss together. Chill for 1 hour before serving.

new potato salad
with balsamic vinegar

		ingredients
extremely easy		1 lb/450 g small new potatoes 2 tbsp balsamic vinegar 6 scallions, sliced thinly salt and pepper
serves 4		
5 minutes		chopped fresh cilantro leaves, to garnish
15 minutes		

Cook the potatoes in salted boiling water for about 15 minutes, or until tender. Drain the cooked potatoes, put in a salad bowl, and let cool slightly.

Add the vinegar, scallions, salt, and pepper to the potatoes and toss together. Serve warm, garnished with cilantro leaves.

spicy harissa
potato salad

		ingredients
	extremely easy	1 lb/450 g small new potatoes
		salt
	serves 4	1 tsp harissa paste
		1 tbsp extra-virgin olive oil
	5 minutes	fresh cilantro leaves, to garnish
	15 minutes	

Cook the potatoes in salted boiling water for about 15 minutes, or until tender. Drain the cooked potatoes, put in a salad bowl, and let cool slightly.

Combine the harissa paste and olive oil. Pour the mixture over the potatoes and toss together. Serve warm, garnished with cilantro.

warm potatoes
with pesto

		ingredients
	extremely easy	1 lb/450 g small new potatoes 3 tsp pesto sauce salt and pepper 1/3 cup freshly grated Parmesan cheese
	serves 4	
	5 minutes	
	15 minutes	

Cook the potatoes in salted boiling water for about 15 minutes, or until tender. Drain, put in a salad bowl, and let cool slightly.

Add the pesto, salt, and pepper to the potatoes and toss together. Sprinkle with the Parmesan cheese and serve warm.

potato wedges
with apricots & walnuts

		ingredients	
extremely easy		2 large potatoes	½ cup ready-to-eat dried
		3 tbsp extra-virgin olive oil	apricots, chopped
		or walnut oil	
serves 4		1 tbsp white wine vinegar	TO SERVE
		large pinch of sugar	salad greens
10 minutes		salt and pepper	1 cup broken walnuts
10 minutes			

Cut each potato into 8 wedges lengthwise. Simmer in a pan with the minimum of salted boiling water for about 10 minutes, or until tender but not falling apart.

Meanwhile, put the oil, white wine vinegar, sugar, salt, and pepper in a screw-topped jar and shake together.

Drain the cooked potatoes and put in a large bowl. Add the apricots, pour in the dressing, and gently toss together.

Arrange the salad greens on a serving dish and add the potato salad. Sprinkle with the walnuts and serve.

hot potato side dishes

A serving of hot, creamy mashed potato, crisp roast potatoes, and good old French fries are the dishes that we rely on every day. You will find them all here, along with some exciting new ideas for side dishes that will complete a main meal and leave you feeling warm and satisfied. There is a mouthwatering range, from Italian Potato Casserole and Cheese Hasselback Potatoes to Sweet-glazed Roast Potatoes and Scalloped Potatoes. In addition, don't forget baking, which has to be the simplest method of cooking potatoes.

italian potato casserole

extremely easy	
serves 4	
10 minutes	
35 minutes	

ingredients

1 lb 12 oz/800 g potatoes, peeled
4 tbsp olive oil
1 onion, thinly sliced
2 tsp chopped garlic
generous 1 cup pitted green
  olives, sliced

1 lb 12 oz/800 g canned
  chopped tomatoes
1 tbsp chopped fresh marjoram
salt and pepper

Cut the potatoes into 1½ inch/4 cm chunks. Heat the oil in a large pan over low heat. Add the potatoes, onion, garlic, and olives and cook for 2–3 minutes over medium heat. Stir in the tomatoes, marjoram, salt, and pepper.

Reduce the heat to very low, cover the pan, and simmer for about 30 minutes, or until the potatoes are tender. Serve hot.

cheese hasselback potatoes

		ingredients	
	very easy		
	serves 4	4 potatoes, peeled 3–4 tbsp sunflower oil salt and pepper ½ cup grated Cheddar cheese	3 tbsp freshly grated Parmesan cheese 2 tbsp chopped fresh chives
	5 minutes		
	1–1¼ hours		

Preheat the oven to 425°F/220°C.

Chop the potatoes into thin slices across their width, cutting three-fourths of the way through.

Put the potatoes in a roasting pan, drizzle with the oil, and season with salt and pepper. Bake in the oven for 50 minutes.

Meanwhile, combine the grated cheeses and chives. Sprinkle the mixture over the potatoes and cook in the oven for a further 10–15 minutes, or until the potatoes are tender and the cheeses have melted and are lightly browned. Serve hot.

roasted garlic
mashed potatoes

		ingredients	
very easy		2 whole bulbs of garlic	½ cup milk
		1 tbsp olive oil	¼ cup butter
serves 4		2 lb/900 g mealy potatoes, peeled	salt and pepper
20 minutes			
1 hour			

Preheat the oven to 350°F/180°C.

Separate the garlic cloves, place on a large piece of foil, and drizzle with the oil. Wrap the garlic in the foil and roast in the oven for about 1 hour, or until very tender. Let cool slightly.

Twenty minutes before the end of the cooking time, cut the potatoes into chunks, then cook in salted boiling water for about 15 minutes, or until tender.

Meanwhile, squeeze the cooled garlic cloves out of their skins and push through a strainer into a pan. Add the milk, butter, salt, and pepper and heat gently, until the butter has melted.

Drain the cooked potatoes, then mash in the pan until smooth. Pour in the garlic mixture and heat gently, stirring, until the ingredients are combined. Serve hot.

sweet-glazed
roast potatoes

		ingredients
extremely easy		4 potatoes, peeled
		salt
serves 4		4 tbsp sunflower oil
		¼ cup butter
		½ cup honey
5 minutes		sprigs of fresh rosemary, to garnish
55 minutes		

Preheat the oven to 350°F/180°C.

Cook the potatoes in salted boiling water for 5 minutes and then drain. Put the potatoes in a roasting pan. Drizzle the oil over the top and put a pat of butter on each potato.

Roast the potatoes in the oven for 30 minutes. Baste the potatoes and then spoon the honey over them. Roast for a further 20 minutes, or until tender. Garnish with the sprigs of fresh rosemary and serve hot.

griddled potato & apple cakes

		ingredients	
easy			
serves 4	12 oz/350 g mealy potatoes, peeled	salt and pepper	
	1 small cooking apple	2 tbsp self-rising flour	
20 minutes	2 tbsp butter	sunflower oil, for brushing	
20–25 minutes			

Cut the potatoes into chunks and then cook in salted boiling water for 15 minutes, or until tender. Meanwhile, peel, core, and chop the apple finely.

When the potatoes are cooked, drain them well and then mash until smooth. Add the butter, salt, and pepper and beat together. Stir in the apple. Add enough flour to make a soft, firm dough.

Divide the dough into 4 equal pieces and shape each piece into a round about ½ inch/1 cm thick.

Cook the potato cakes on a hot griddle (brushed with sunflower oil) for 5–10 minutes, turning once, until they are an even golden brown. Serve hot.

roast vegetables
with fresh herbs

extremely easy	
serves 4	
5 minutes	
1–1½ hours	

ingredients

1 lb/450 g potatoes, peeled
1 lb/450 g red onions, peeled
3 tbsp olive oil

3 tbsp lemon juice
6 tbsp chopped fresh herbs, such as
  rosemary, thyme, and sage

Preheat the oven to 400°F/200°C.

Cut the potatoes and onions into fourths and put in a roasting pan. Add all the remaining ingredients and toss together.

Cover the pan and roast in the oven for 1–1½ hours, stirring once or twice, until the vegetables are tender and golden brown. Remove from the oven and serve immediately.

scalloped potatoes

		ingredients
	extremely easy	¼ cup butter
		1 lb 8 oz/675 g potatoes, peeled
	serves 4	salt and pepper
		3 tbsp all-purpose white flour
		⅔ cup milk
	10 minutes	1 tbsp chopped fresh parsley, to serve
	1 ¼ hours	

Preheat the oven to 375°F/190°C. Grease an ovenproof dish with some of the butter.

Thinly slice the potatoes and arrange them in layers in the dish. Add salt and pepper, sprinkle with flour, and dot with the remaining butter. When all the slices have been used, pour the milk over the top.

Bake in the oven for about 1¼ hours, until the potatoes are cooked and their tops are golden brown. Remove from the oven, sprinkle with chopped parsley, and serve immediately.

indian spinach
& potatoes

		ingredients	
very easy			
		1 lb/450 g frozen leaf spinach, thawed and drained	2 garlic cloves, crushed
serves 4		1 lb/450 g potatoes, peeled	2 tsp ground coriander
		4 tbsp vegetable oil	¼ tsp cayenne pepper
		2 tsp whole black mustard seeds	pinch of salt
		1 onion, sliced thinly	⅔ cup water
10 minutes			
30 minutes			

Put the spinach in a pan and heat very gently for about 5 minutes, stirring occasionally, to dry off as much liquid as possible. Meanwhile, thinly slice the potatoes.

Heat the oil in a large skillet, add the mustard seeds, and cook for a few seconds, or until they begin to pop. Add the onion and garlic and cook for about 5 minutes, stirring frequently, until the onion starts to brown.

Stir in the potatoes, coriander, cayenne, and salt and cook for 1 minute. Add the water, bring to a boil, then simmer for 10 minutes, stirring occasionally.

Stir in the spinach and simmer for a further 10 minutes, or until the potatoes are tender. Serve hot.

homemade oven french fries

		ingredients
extremely easy		1 lb/450 g potatoes, peeled
		2 tbsp sunflower oil
serves 4		salt and pepper
10 minutes		
40–45 minutes		

Preheat the oven to 400°F/200°C.

Cut the potatoes into thick, even-sized sticks. Rinse them under cold running water and then dry well on a clean dish towel. Put in a bowl, add the oil, and toss together until coated.

Spread the fries on a cookie sheet and cook in the oven for 40–45 minutes, turning once, until golden. Add salt and pepper to taste, and serve hot.

thai new potatoes

extremely easy	
serves 4	
10 minutes	
15 minutes	

ingredients

1 lb/450 g new potatoes
1 tbsp vegetable oil
2 tbsp butter
1 tsp chopped ginger root
1 tsp chopped garlic

1 red chile, seeded and chopped finely
salt and pepper

fresh cilantro leaves, to garnish

Cut any large potatoes in half, then cook in salted boiling water for about 15 minutes, or until tender. Drain, turn into a serving dish, and let cool slightly.

Heat the oil and butter in a skillet. Add the ginger, garlic and chile and cook for 4–5 minutes, or until the chile has softened.

Spoon the mixture over the potatoes, add salt and pepper, and toss together. Serve garnished with cilantro leaves.

light potato lunches

Often, all you need to eat at lunchtime or at other times of the day, is something light and easy to prepare. The potato is an invaluable ingredient for a midday snack or light meal. Omelets, pizzas, pancakes, and salads are all dishes that fall into this category and potatoes can be included in any of them. In this chapter, you will find a variety of delicious recipes to brighten up your lunches, inspired by traditional dishes from Europe and America.

cherry tomato & potato salad with feta cheese

		ingredients	
easy		1 lb/450 g small new potatoes	salt and pepper
		3 tbsp extra-virgin olive oil	16 cherry tomatoes, halved
serves 4		1 tbsp white wine vinegar	½ cup feta cheese, cubed
		½ tsp sugar	scant ½ cup chopped walnuts
15 minutes			
15 minutes			

Cook the potatoes in salted boiling water for about 15 minutes, or until tender. Remove from the heat, drain, and put in a salad bowl. Let cool slightly.

Meanwhile, to make the dressing, put the oil, vinegar, and sugar in a screw-topped jar and shake together. Season to taste, then replace the lid, and shake well.

Add the tomato halves, cheese, and walnuts to the potatoes and toss together. Pour the dressing over the salad and toss again. Serve warm.

stir-fried chicken & potato salad

		ingredients	
easy		MARINADE	DRESSING
		2 tbsp olive oil	2 tbsp olive oil
		1 tbsp lime juice	1 tbsp lime juice
serves 4		1 garlic clove, crushed	2 tsp wholegrain mustard
		salt and pepper	salt and pepper
15 minutes + 1 hour to marinate		4 skinless, boneless chicken breast portions	1 tbsp olive oil, for frying
20–30 minutes		1 lb/450 g new potatoes, cut into fourths	salad greens, to serve

To make the marinade, put the olive oil, lime juice, garlic, salt, and pepper in a bowl and mix together. Cut the chicken into thin strips and add to the marinade. Cover and let marinate in the refrigerator for about 1 hour.

Meanwhile, cook the potatoes in salted boiling water for about 15 minutes, or until tender, then drain. To make the dressing, put the oil, lime juice, mustard, salt, and pepper in a screw-topped jar.

Heat 1 tablespoon of olive oil in a wok or large skillet, add the chicken and marinade, and stir-fry for 10–15 minutes, or until the chicken is cooked. Add the potatoes and stir-fry for 1 minute.

Put the salad greens in a salad bowl. Shake the dressing ingredients in the jar and pour it over the greens. Toss the salad, top with the chicken and potatoes, and serve.

potato skins
with tomato & corn salsa

		ingredients	
easy		2 large baking potatoes	1 red chile, seeded and chopped finely
		2 tbsp olive oil, plus extra for brushing	1 tbsp chopped fresh cilantro leaves
serves 4		2 large tomatoes, diced	1 tbsp lime juice
		and seeded	salt and pepper
		½ cup corn kernels	½ cup grated Cheddar cheese
20 minutes		scant ½ cup canned navy beans	
		2 shallots, sliced thinly	
		¼ red bell pepper, diced finely	
1 hour 10 minutes			

Preheat the oven to 400°F/200°C.

Pierce the potatoes in several places with a knife, then brush with oil. Cook directly on the oven shelf for about 1 hour, or until tender.

Meanwhile, make the salsa. In a bowl, combine the oil, tomatoes, corn, navy beans, shallots, red bell pepper, chile, cilantro, lime juice, salt, and pepper.

When the potatoes are cooked, cut them in half and, using a teaspoon, scoop out the flesh, leaving the skin intact. Brush the insides with oil, then place on a cookie sheet, cut side up. Cook under a preheated broiler for about 5 minutes, or until crisp.

Spoon the salsa into the potato skins and sprinkle the cheese over the top. Return the potato skins to the broiler and cook gently until the cheese has melted. Serve hot.

frittata with bacon & vegetables

easy	
serves 4	
10 minutes	
20–30 minutes	

ingredients

6 eggs
1 cup grated Cheddar cheese
1 tbsp chopped fresh cilantro leaves
salt and pepper
2 tbsp sunflower oil
3 tbsp butter
1 onion, chopped

1 zucchini, sliced thinly
1 tsp chopped garlic
1⅓ cups diced bacon
1½ cups cooked potatoes, diced

Beat the eggs in a bowl and stir in the cheese. Add the chopped cilantro, salt, and pepper.

Heat the oil and butter in a large skillet, then add the onion, zucchini, garlic, and bacon, and cook for 5–10 minutes, or until softened. Add the potatoes and cook for a further 5–10 minutes, or until they are lightly browned.

Pour in the egg mixture. Cook over low heat for 5–10 minutes, or until all but the top of the mixture is set.

Transfer the skillet to a preheated broiler and cook until the top is set, but not hard. Serve the frittata hot, cut into wedges.

hash browns

		ingredients
easy		

1 lb/450 g potatoes, peeled
4 tbsp sunflower oil
1 onion, chopped
4 bacon strips, chopped roughly
1²⁄₃ cups white mushrooms, halved

1 red or green bell pepper, seeded
    and chopped roughly
salt and pepper

chopped fresh parsley, to garnish
chili sauce or ketchup, to serve

serves 4

15 minutes

25 minutes

Grate the potatoes, then rinse them under cold running water until the water runs clear. Squeeze out the water and dry the potatoes in a clean dish towel.

Heat the oil in a large, heavy skillet, then add the potatoes, and cook, stirring frequently, for 8–10 minutes, or until beginning to turn brown. Add the onion, bacon, mushrooms, salt and pepper, and red or green bell pepper, then continue to cook, stirring frequently, for a further 15 minutes, or until the mixture is golden brown.

Garnish with parsley and serve hot, with chili sauce or ketchup.

spanish omelet

easy	
serves 4	
10 minutes	
25–35 minutes	

ingredients

6 eggs
4 tbsp milk
salt and pepper
1 lb/450 g potatoes, peeled
2 tbsp olive oil
2 tbsp butter

2 onions, chopped finely
1 green or red bell pepper, seeded,
   and chopped finely

chopped fresh flat leaf parsley,
   to garnish

In a bowl, beat together the eggs, milk, salt, and pepper.
Cut the potatoes into ½ inch/1 cm cubes.

Heat the oil and butter in a large skillet. Add the potatoes, onions, and the red or green bell pepper, and cook very slowly for 10–15 minutes, stirring occasionally, until almost cooked. Raise the heat and cook for a further 5–10 minutes, until the vegetables start to brown.

Pour in the egg mixture and cook over a low heat for 5 minutes, or until the mixture is set and the underside is golden brown.

Transfer the skillet to a preheated broiler and cook until the top is set and golden brown. Garnish the omelet with parsley and serve it hot, cut into wedges.

italian potato bread

		ingredients	
easy		12 oz/350 g mealy potatoes, peeled	2 tbsp olive oil
		salt and pepper	½ cup mozzarella cheese,
serves 4		6 cups white bread flour	thinly sliced
		1 envelope active dry yeast	
		⅔ cup grated Parmesan cheese	rosemary, to garnish
20 minutes + 1 hour to rise		1 tsp finely chopped rosemary leaves	
		large pinch of grated nutmeg	fresh tomatoes, to serve
		2 cups warm water	
55 minutes			

Cut the potatoes into chunks, then cook in salted boiling water for 15 minutes, or until tender. Drain well, then mash until smooth.

Put the mashed potato in a large bowl and mix in the flour, 2 teaspoons of the salt, the yeast, Parmesan cheese, rosemary, nutmeg, and pepper. Add the water and mix together to form a smooth dough.

On a floured surface, knead the dough for about 5 minutes. Roll out to form a 10 inch/25 cm round and place on a cookie sheet. Cover with a clean dish towel and let rise in a warm place for about 1 hour, or until doubled in size.

Preheat the oven to 400°F/200°C. Brush the dough with the oil and bake in the oven for 30 minutes. Top with the mozzarella cheese and return the bread to the oven for 10 minutes, or until golden brown. Garnish with rosemary and serve with tomatoes.

crisp onion
& potato pancakes

easy	
serves 4	
15 minutes	
12–20 minutes	

ingredients

1 lb/450 g potatoes, peeled
2 shallots
4 scallions, sliced thinly
1 tsp chopped garlic

1 egg, beaten
salt and pepper
2–4 tbsp all-purpose white flour
vegetable oil, for shallow frying

Grate the potatoes and shallots. Drain off excess liquid, then put the mixture in a large bowl.

Add the scallions, garlic, egg, salt and pepper, and enough flour to make a thick batter.

In a large skillet, heat enough oil to cover the bottom. Drop spoonfuls of the mixture into the skillet to form pancakes measuring about 3 inches/7.5 cm wide and ½ inch/1 cm thick. Cook for 3–5 minutes on each side, or until the pancakes are golden brown. Drain the pancakes on paper towels. Repeat the process to form more pancakes, until all the potato mixture has been used. Serve hot.

garlic potatoes
with goat cheese

		ingredients
easy		2 lb/900 g potatoes, peeled
		6 tbsp butter
serves 4		1 tsp chopped garlic
		salt and pepper
		½ cup goat cheese, sliced thinly
25 minutes		
30–35 minutes		

Preheat the oven to 400°F/200°C.

Thinly slice the potatoes. Melt the butter and then add the garlic, salt, and pepper. Use the mixture to coat the potatoes and arrange them on a greased cookie sheet, overlapping to form 8 x 4 inch/10 cm rounds.

Cook the potatoes in the oven for 25 minutes. Arrange the cheese on top of the potatoes and return them to the oven for a further 5–10 minutes, or until the cheese is bubbling. Serve hot.

swiss rösti fish cakes

		ingredients	
easy		1 lb/450 g cod fillet, skinned	salt and pepper
		4 tbsp chopped fresh parsley	12 oz/350 g potatoes, peeled
serves 4		1 egg, beaten	vegetable oil, for shallow frying
25 minutes			
12–16 minutes			

Cut the fish into chunks and put in a food processor with the parsley, egg, salt, and pepper. Process until the fish is coarsely ground and the ingredients are mixed.

Grate the potatoes, squeeze out the excess liquid, and then dry in a clean dish towel. Put on a large plate and add salt and pepper.

Divide the fish mixture into 8 equal balls, then roll these in the grated potato. Flatten slightly with the palm of your hand.

In a large skillet, heat enough oil to cover the bottom. Cook the fish cakes, in batches, for 3–4 minutes on each side, or until golden brown. Drain on paper towels. Continue until all the fish cakes have been cooked. Serve hot.

easy suppers with potatoes

For the main meal of the day, whatever time it is eaten, something nourishing and substantial is needed. This chapter includes recipes that are easy to make and delicious to eat and that will leave you feeling satisfied. Baked potatoes with various fillings, mouthwatering fish dishes, and even the traditional Shepherd's Pie are all included here. Several could even be served for an informal supper party. The recipes also show how flexible and convenient potatoes can be. Most of the dishes will need only salad greens to accompany them.

baked potatoes with sichuan chicken

		ingredients
easy	4 large baking potatoes	8 oz/225 g canned water chestnuts,
	4 tbsp vegetable oil	drained and sliced
serves 4	3 boneless chicken breast portions,	1 tbsp cornstarch
	sliced thinly	2 tbsp Sichuan sauce (or soy sauce,
	4 scallions, sliced thinly	if unavailable)
20 minutes	2 carrots, sliced very thinly	generous 1 cup water
	1 green bell pepper, seeded and diced	
	2 cups Napa cabbage or Savoy	
1–1¼ hours	cabbage, chopped	

Preheat the oven to 400°F/200°C.

Pierce the potatoes with a knife in several places. Cook directly on the oven shelf for about 1 hour, or until tender.

About 15 minutes before the potatoes are cooked, heat the oil in a wok or large skillet. Add the chicken and stir-fry for 5 minutes, or until browned.

Add the scallions, carrots, and green bell pepper and stir-fry for 2–3 minutes. Add the cabbage and water chestnuts and stir-fry for 2–3 minutes, or until the vegetables are almost tender.

Blend the cornstarch with the Sichuan sauce and water. Pour into the wok, bring to a boil, and turn down the heat to medium. Cook, stirring, for 2–3 minutes, or until the chicken is tender.

Cut the cooked potatoes in half and serve with the Sichuan chicken spooned over the top.

potato gnocchi

	ingredients	
easy	2 lb/900 g mealy potatoes, peeled	TO SERVE
	1 tsp salt	tomato sauce or pesto
serves 4	1 tbsp olive oil	grated Parmesan cheese
	2–2½ cups all-purpose white flour	
	1 tsp baking powder	
25 minutes	1 egg, beaten	
20 minutes		

Cut the potatoes into chunks and cook in salted boiling water for 15 minutes, or until tender. Drain well, then push through a strainer into a large bowl. Mix in the oil.

Stir together the flour, 1 teaspoon of salt, and the baking powder. Add half to the potatoes, with the egg, and mix together. Gradually knead in the remaining flour to form a smooth, slightly sticky dough.

On a floured surface, shape the dough into 1 inch/2.5 cm thick rolls, then cut into ¾ inch/2 cm pieces. Using the prongs of a fork, roll each piece toward you to curl in the sides and mark the top.

Bring a large pan of water to a boil, then reduce to a simmer. Add about 30 gnocchi and cook for 1–2 minutes, until they float to the surface. Repeat until all the gnocchi are cooked.

To serve, toss the gnocchi in the tomato or pesto sauce and sprinkle with Parmesan cheese.

garlic-crusted
roast haddock

easy	
serves 4	
15 minutes	
25–27 minutes	

ingredients

2 lb/900 g mealy potatoes, peeled
½ cup milk
¼ cup butter
salt and pepper
4 x 8 oz/225 g haddock fillets

1 tbsp sunflower oil
4 garlic cloves, chopped finely

2 tbsp chopped fresh parsley,
  to garnish

Preheat the oven to 450°F/230°C.

Cut the potatoes into chunks and cook in salted boiling water for 15 minutes, or until tender. Drain well, then mash in the pan until smooth. Over low heat, beat in the milk, butter, salt, and pepper.

Put the haddock fillets in a roasting pan and brush the fish with the oil. Sprinkle the garlic on top, add salt and pepper, then spread with the mashed potatoes. Roast in the oven for 8–10 minutes, or until the fish is just tender.

Meanwhile, preheat the broiler. Transfer the fish to the broiler and cook for about 2 minutes, or until golden brown. Sprinkle with the chopped parsley and serve immediately.

shepherd's pie

very easy	
serves 4	
15 minutes	
45 minutes	

ingredients

2 lb/900 g mealy potatoes, peeled
12 oz/350 g cold roast lamb, ground
1 onion, chopped finely
2 tbsp all-purpose white flour
1 tbsp tomato paste

1 $\frac{1}{4}$ cups vegetable bouillon
2 tbsp chopped fresh parsley
salt and pepper
4 tbsp milk
2 tbsp butter

Preheat the oven to 350°F/180°C.

Cut the potatoes into chunks and cook in salted boiling water for 15 minutes, or until tender.

Meanwhile, put the lamb, onion, flour, tomato paste, bouillon, parsley, salt, and pepper in a bowl and mix together. Turn out the mixture into an ovenproof dish.

Drain the cooked potatoes, then mash in the pan until smooth. Over low heat, beat in the milk, butter, salt, and pepper until well mixed. Spoon on top of the lamb. Mark the top with a fork.

Bake in the oven for about 30 minutes, or until golden brown. Serve immediately.

baked potatoes
with tuna & apple

		ingredients	
very easy		4 large baking potatoes	2 celery stalks, sliced thinly
		vegetable oil, for brushing	½ cup mayonnaise
serves 4		1 tbsp lemon juice	½ cup crème fraîche
		2 eating apples	1 tsp wholegrain mustard
		6 oz/175 g canned tuna chunks in oil,	salt and pepper
15 minutes		drained and flaked	
1 hour			

Preheat the oven to 400°F/200°C.

Pierce the potatoes with a knife in several places, then brush with oil. Cook directly on the oven shelf for about 1 hour, or until tender.

Meanwhile, put the lemon juice in a bowl. Core and chop the apples, then add them to the lemon juice, and toss well to coat the apple pieces. Add the tuna, celery, mayonnaise, crème fraîche, mustard, salt, and pepper and toss together.

When the potatoes are cooked, cut them in half and serve with the tuna mixture spooned over the top.

baked salmon & potatoes with mustard sauce

easy	**ingredients**	
serves 4	1 lb 8 oz/675 g potatoes, peeled 4 tbsp sunflower oil 4 x 6 oz/175 g salmon fillets 1 tbsp lemon juice	2 tbsp butter salt and pepper ½ cup heavy cream 2 tsp Dijon mustard
15 minutes		
25 minutes		

Preheat the oven to 450°F/230°C.

Cut the potatoes into ½ inch/1 cm dice, then cook in salted boiling water for 2 minutes. Drain and put in a roasting pan. Add the oil and toss together. Bake in the oven for 15 minutes.

Meanwhile, put the salmon fillets in an ovenproof dish. Drizzle with lemon juice, top each fillet with a pat of butter, and season with salt and pepper.

Toss the potatoes and return to the oven with the salmon. Bake for 10 minutes, or until the salmon is tender.

Meanwhile, in a small pan, gently heat the cream. Remove from the heat and add the mustard, salt, and pepper. Serve the salmon and potatoes with the sauce poured over.

chicken hash
with fried eggs

easy	
serves 4	
10 minutes	
30 minutes	

ingredients

2 lb/900 g mealy potatoes, peeled
4 skinless, boneless chicken
   breast portions
2 tbsp vegetable oil
1 onion, chopped finely

1 garlic clove, chopped finely
salt and pepper
2 tbsp chopped fresh parsley
4 eggs

Cut the potatoes into ¾ inch/2 cm dice and cook in salted boiling water for 5 minutes, or until just tender. Drain well.

Cut the chicken into ¾ inch/2 cm pieces. Heat half the oil in a large skillet. Add the onion and garlic and cook, stirring, for about 5 minutes, or until the onion has softened. Add the chicken, salt, and pepper and cook, stirring, for a further 5 minutes, or until the onion and chicken have browned.

Add the drained potatoes and cook, stirring occasionally, for 10 minutes, or until the potatoes have browned. Stir in the parsley.

Meanwhile, in a separate skillet, heat the remaining oil. Break the eggs individually into the hot fat and cook until set.

Serve the chicken hash topped with a cooked egg.

pan-fried liver & bacon with potato cakes

easy	
serves 4	
20 minutes	
20–30 minutes	

ingredients

1 lb/450 g potatoes, peeled
1 egg, beaten
4 tbsp all-purpose white flour,
  plus extra for dusting
salt and pepper

1 lb/450 g sliced lamb's liver
sunflower oil, for frying
4 bacon strips
2 onions, sliced thinly

Grate the potatoes, then rinse under cold running water until the water runs clear. Squeeze out the water and dry the potatoes in a clean dish towel. Put the potatoes in a large bowl and add the egg, flour, salt, and pepper and mix well together.

Dust the liver with flour and add salt and pepper.

Heat about ¼ inch/5 mm oil in a large skillet, then add large tablespoons of the potato mixture, flattening them with a spatula. Cook for about 10 minutes, turning once, until golden brown. Remove from the skillet and keep hot. Continue until all the mixture has been cooked.

In a separate skillet, heat enough oil to cover the bottom. Add the bacon and cook until crisp, then push to one side. Add the onions and cook for 5 minutes, or until browned. Push to one side of the skillet, add the liver, and cook for 6–8 minutes, turning once, until tender. Serve with the potato cakes.

index